W9-BOO-521

# Stories
## of
# Thor

## Three Norse Myths

Adapted by Alex Frith

Illustrated by Natasha Kuricheva

Reading consultant: Alison Kelly

# The people and places in this book

**Asgard**, *say* Az-guard – the land of the gods

**Freya**, *rhymes with* player – the goddess of love and beauty

**Geirrod**, *say* Gay-rod – a frost giant

**Gjalp**, *say* Geeyalp – daughter of Geirrod

**Greip**, *say* Gripe – daughter of Geirrod

**Grid**, *rhymes with* lid – a friendly giant

**Hymir**, *say* High-mere – a stone giant, married to Tyr's mother

**Jormungand**, *say* Your-moon-gand – a gigantic sea serpent

**Jotunheim**, *say* Your-tun-hime –
the land of the giants

**Loki**, *say* Low-key – god of mischief
and Thor's stepbrother

**Mjolnir**, *say* M-yol-near – Thor's
magical hammer

**Odin**, *say* Oh-dinn – the king of the
gods and Thor's father

**Thor**, *rhymes with* sore – the god of
thunder and lightning

**Thrym**, *rhymes with* him – the king of
the cave giants

**Tyr**, *like the outside of a car wheel* –
the god of battle (whose right hand was
bitten off by a wolf)

**Valhalla**, *say* Val-hal-uh – the feasting
hall of the gods

# Contents

# Chapter 1

# Thor and the sea serpent

In Valhalla, the great hall of the gods, everyone was preparing for a grand feast. "I want something HUGE and special to hold our drink," bellowed Odin, king of the gods. "Who can bring me a pot large enough?"

"My stepfather, Hymir, has one," said Tyr, the god of battle. "But he won't lend it." Hymir was a fearsome giant. Even Tyr was afraid of him.

Then Odin's son, Thor, strode up. "I'll get you that pot, Father," he boasted.

"I'd like to see you try," said Tyr.

The pot was so vast that it
sat outside Hymir's house.
"How will you get it?" Tyr asked.
"I don't know," admitted Thor.
"Maybe I'll fight Hymir for it."

Tyr laughed. Thor was one of
the strongest gods, but he wasn't
stronger than a giant... Was he?

Before they could make a better
plan, Tyr's mother opened the door.
"You're just in time for supper!"
she said with a smile.

Hymir was already at the table.
"Hello," said Thor, as he came in.
"May I borrow your giant pot?"
"NO!" roared Hymir.

Thor shrugged and began to munch on an ox.

Hymir growled in fury.

"May I borrow your pot?" asked Thor again, with his mouth full.

"What about a contest for it?" Tyr broke in, seeing Hymir leap up.

"Hmm..." said Hymir. "We'll go fishing tomorrow. If you catch more than me, I *might* lend it."

Just after dawn, Hymir and Thor climbed into Hymir's fishing boat. Thor had brought a large sack along with him.

What does he have in there?

When they had rowed far out to sea, Hymir threw in his net and waited. Soon, he had caught two enormous whales.

"Look at my haul!" he bragged, holding up the writhing beasts. "And you haven't caught a thing."

"We need to row out further," said Thor. "I'll still beat you easily."

While Hymir rowed, Thor opened his sack. Inside was an ox head, left over from supper the night before. Thor tied it to a fishing line and hurled it out to sea.

Within seconds, Thor felt a tug
on the line. He tried to pull it
in, but it wouldn't move.

He pulled harder... and harder...
Hymir laughed. "Poor little god,
is it too heavy for you?" he taunted.

Thor pushed his feet against the boat and pulled with all his might.

At last, the line rose up out of the water. Caught on the end was a gigantic sea serpent.

"That's Jormungand!" cried Hymir. "He's too big. Let go!"

The serpent was so vast, it could keep its tail on the ocean floor and hoist its neck above the waves.

I am Thor, son of Odin! You will not beat me!

As Thor struggled, the weather started to change. Dark clouds gathered and a storm blew up. Lightning cracked in the sky. Giant waves rocked the boat.

Thor reached for his magical hammer, Mjolnir, and brought it crashing down on the serpent's head. The creature slumped onto the boat, smashing a hole in it.

"We're capsizing!" screamed Hymir. He grabbed his harpoon and cut through the fishing line.

Thor toppled back. Jormungand slid beneath the water.

The storm began to calm, but Hymir was panicking. The boat was sinking and he couldn't swim.

"We're done for," he moaned.

"Don't worry," said Thor. He dived into the sea, grabbed hold of the boat and began to swim.

Hymir couldn't believe it. Thor was pulling him, the boat *and* the two whales. He swam with them all the way to shore.

"*Now* may I borrow your pot?" Thor asked Hymir, when they finally reached the house. "Or shall we fight for it?"

Hymir looked horrified. "I'm not fighting *you*. You may borrow the pot if you can break this." And he handed Thor a glass goblet.

Thor threw the goblet at the ground. It bounced. He tried again. This time, he hurled it with all his strength at a pillar.

The pillar smashed into tiny pieces, but the goblet stayed whole. Thor didn't know it, but it was an enchanted goblet, tougher than any stone.

"If this carries on, Thor will wreck the house," thought Tyr's mother. "I'd better tell him the secret."

She whispered in Thor's ear. "The hardest thing here is my husband's head. Throw the goblet at that."

Thor threw it hard at Hymir, and the goblet finally shattered.

Hey!

"Now may I have the pot?" asked Thor, grinning.

"All right," snapped Hymir.
Thor smiled and held it high over his head in triumph.

"I have one last challenge for you, Thor," said Tyr, as they headed home. "Race you to the feast!"

# Chapter 2

# Thor loses his hammer

Thor loved his hammer, Mjolnir, so much, that he even took it to bed with him. Then, one terrible morning, he woke to find it missing.

"Where is Mjolnir?" he thundered. "Some thief has taken my hammer. He will pay!"

Furious, Thor jumped out of bed, howling with rage. He didn't know who had stolen his hammer, but he had a good idea – his stepbrother, Loki, god of mischief.

"Where's my hammer, ferret face?" bellowed Thor.

"Dear brother, I've no idea," Loki whimpered.

"Don't you dare lie to me, villain!"

You thief!

"I'm not lying, I promise," said Loki. "I may enjoy playing tricks, but I wouldn't dare steal Mjolnir."

Loki saw Thor was about to explode with anger. "I'll help you catch the thief," he promised. "Come with me."

Loki led Thor to see Freya, the goddess of love.

"Freya wouldn't steal!" said Thor. "In fact, men keep giving her gifts."

"Exactly," said Loki. "It's one of those gifts we need."

Greetings, beautiful Freya.

"Greetings, mischievous Loki," said Freya. "What tricks have you come to play today?"

"No tricks, Freya. This is serious. Someone has stolen Thor's hammer. May I borrow your magical cloak so I can fly off to find it?"

"If it will help Thor," said Freya, smiling at them, "of course you may borrow my cloak."

The instant Loki put it on, the cloak transformed. Spreading his new wings, Loki rose into the sky.

He flew all the way into Jotunheim, until he spied Mjolnir glinting in the sunlight. It was lying in the mouth of a cave.

Loki swooped down, but as he touched the hammer, two thick hands grabbed him.

The god caught a glimpse of his captor – a craggy, blue-skinned cave giant – before he was plunged into darkness.

33

The giant dragged him, kicking and struggling, deep underground. Loki was in the palace of Thrym, king of the cave giants.

Thrym sneered at his captive. "I'll make you a deal, puny god," he growled. "Bring me Freya as my bride. Once we are married, I'll return Thor's hammer."

Loki pretended to shake with
fear. "I'll do it," he promised.
Secretly, he was hatching a plan
to trick King Thrym in return.

"Then go!" said Thrym. "Bring
Freya to me in one week."

Loki flew straight
back to Freya's house.

"I've found Mjolnir," he
told Thor proudly, "but I couldn't
bring it back. King Thrym has it."

"I knew it!" yelled Thor. "Those ugly, cave-dwelling wretches are always making trouble. I'll sort out the lot of them!"

"Calm down," said Loki. "You can't just walk into the palace unarmed. But we have something he wants. King Thrym wishes to marry Freya."

"Marry *me?*" said Freya. "I'd never marry a cave giant!"

"Don't worry, Freya," said Loki. "We'll dress Thor in your clothes, give him your necklace and send him to Thrym in your place!"

WHAT?

I'll go too, disguised as a bridesmaid.

Exactly one week later, Thor
and Loki arrived at King Thrym's
court, dressed for the wedding.

Thor's face was covered in a veil,
but everyone could see Freya's
famous necklace hanging around
his neck. His disguise was working.

Thrym had put on a magnificent
banquet but he was too excited to
eat. He gazed at his bride-to-be.
She had no trouble eating. In fact,
she polished off two whole oxen.

Thrym began to suspect a trick. He summoned the bridesmaid.

"What is the matter with Freya?" he asked. "I've never seen a woman eat so much food so fast."

Loki was ready with a reply. "The thing is, great king, Freya was so excited about the wedding that she hasn't eaten all week."

"In that case," roared Thrym, "let the ceremony begin!"

Thor walked slowly to the front of the court and waited for King Thrym. He knew the disguise wouldn't fool the king much longer.

Thrym ripped off Thor's veil, revealing his face. Quickly, Thor reached to the throne in front of him, grabbed his hammer...

...and brought it crashing down on Thrym's head. He hit him again and again, forcing the stunned king to the ground.

Loki pulled Thor away and the two gods tore from the court, up to the open air and home.

Back in Asgard, the gods laughed to see Thor in Freya's wedding dress. Freya wasn't laughing.

"Where's my necklace?" she demanded.

"Oh... Thrym must have it," said Thor. "But don't worry," he added. "I can fight my way into his palace and get it for you, now that I have my hammer back!"

# Chapter 3

# Thor's magical weapons

Loki was up to mischief. He had stolen Freya's magical cloak and was flying to Jotunheim, planning to spy on the frost giants, bitter enemies of the gods.

Feeling tired, he swooped down to rest on an icy peak... which let out an angry roar.

Loki gulped.

He had just landed on Geirrod, a massive, ugly frost giant.

"Hey!" cried Geirrod, grabbing Loki in his gigantic hands. "How dare you land on me!"

"Please let me go," begged Loki, thinking fast, "or my stepbrother, Thor, will come looking for me. And then you'll be sorry!"

"I've always wanted to fight that arrogant god," said Geirrod. "But he cheats. He uses a magic hammer."

"If you let me fly home," Loki said quickly, "I'll persuade Thor to come here – without his hammer."

"Go on then," grunted Geirrod.
Soon, a relieved Loki was back in
Asgard, up to his tricks with Thor.

"I couldn't outfight Geirrod,"
said Loki. "I'm not sure even *you*
could. And you definitely couldn't
defeat him without your hammer."

Thor couldn't resist the challenge. He put on a thick cloak and set out for Jotunheim and the icy mountain where Geirrod lived.

Days later, Thor had almost reached Geirrod's castle when a blizzard whirled up around him.

Blinking against the snow, he fought his way to a nearby hut and knocked on the door.

The door swung open... to reveal
a frost giantess, cooking soup in a
vast cauldron.

"Come in, little god," she said.
"I'm Grid. I won't harm you. But
tell me, what are you doing here?"

"I've come to fight Geirrod," boasted Thor. "Um, just as soon as this blizzard dies down."

Grid laughed, before looking serious. "That mean frost giant deserves everything he gets," she said. "But you'll need some help."

"Geirrod is bound to cheat," she explained, "and his daughters Gjalp and Greip will help him. You'll need magical weapons."

She rummaged in a cupboard and handed some things to Thor.

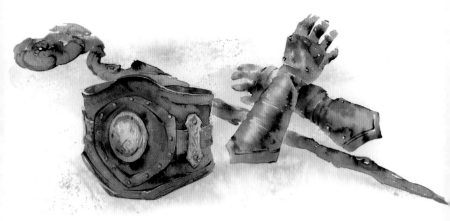

"Here you are... This wooden staff is unbreakable. These iron gloves will protect your hands and the belt will double your strength."

Armed with his new weapons, Thor headed into the cold once more. Geirrod's castle lay ahead but to reach it he had to wade through a deep river.

55

Halfway across, he felt the icy
water rising up above his waist.
Thor looked over to the river bank.

Gjalp, one of Geirrod's daughters,
was using a flaming torch to melt
the ice on a tree. With every second,
the river grew deeper.

Thor felt the river starting to
swallow him up. In desperation,
he grasped a massive rock.

The magical belt made him
so strong, he could lift it. Grunting,
he hurled the rock at Gjalp.

Gjalp went flying with a startled cry and Thor waded to the bank as fast as he could. Throwing off his soaking-wet cloak, he charged into Geirrod's castle.

The castle seemed deserted,
so Thor wandered to an empty
chair and sat down to wait. To his
astonishment, he felt the chair rise
into the air.

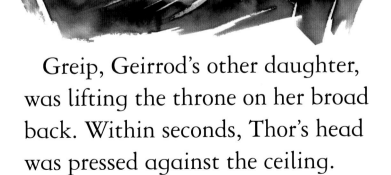

Greip, Geirrod's other daughter,
was lifting the throne on her broad
back. Within seconds, Thor's head
was pressed against the ceiling.

Thor gripped the unbreakable staff with both hands and wedged it between the ceiling and the chair.

Greip pushed and pushed, but the staff held strong.

"Aaagh," Greip groaned at last, collapsing to the floor. Thor and the chair came crashing down.

Thor clambered to his feet and saw a blur of movement. He dived back to the floor, just as a flaming red rock flew past.

Looking up, Thor found himself face to face with Geirrod. The ferocious giant was holding a huge pair of tongs. He thrust them into a bubbling cauldron, drew out another burning rock and threw it.

Quicker than a blink, Thor pulled
on the gloves and caught the rock
as it hurtled at his face. He flung it
back as hard as he could...

...and watched as it punched a
hole through the frost giant's chest.
Geirrod was dead.

Thor strode back to Asgard in triumph.

"This calls for a feast!" cried Odin, when he saw his son.

Once again, the god of thunder had come out on top.

# Usborne Quicklinks

To find links to websites about Thor and life in
Viking times, when these myths were told, and for a
pronunciation guide to the names in this book,
go to the Usborne Quicklinks Website at
**www.usborne.com/quicklinks** and type in
the keywords 'Stories of Thor'.

Please follow the internet safety guidelines at the
Usborne Quicklinks website. Usborne Publishing cannot
be responsible for any website other than its own.

Norse expert: Katrina Johnson
Designed by Sam Whibley
Series editor: Lesley Sims
Series designer: Russell Punter

First published in 2016 by Usborne Publishing Ltd., Usborne House,
83-85 Saffron Hill, London EC1N 8RT, England. www.usborne.com

Copyright © 2016 Usborne Publishing Ltd. All rights reserved.
No part of this publication may be reproduced, stored in a retrieval
system or transmitted in any form or by any means, electronic,
mechanical, photocopying, recording or otherwise, without the prior
permission of the publisher. The name Usborne and the devices ♀ ⊕ are
Trade Marks of Usborne Publishing Ltd. UE.